FLASHES OF GENIUS

Original title: Darwin e la vera storia dei dinosauri

Texts and illustrations by Luca Novelli

Graphic design by Studio Link (www.studio-link.it)

Copyright © 2000 Luca Novelli/Quipos

Copyright © 2001, 2009 Editoriale Scienza S.r.l., Firenze –Trieste

www.editorialescienza.it

www.giunti.it

English edition published in the USA by

Chicago Review Press Incorporated

814 North Franklin Street

Chicago, Illinois 60610

ISBN 978-1-61373-873-3

Library of Congress Cataloging-in-Publication Data

Is available from the Library of Congress.

Printed in the United States of America

5 4 3 2 1

Luca Novelli

Darwin
and the True Story
of the Dinosaurs

CHICAGO
REVIEW
PRESS

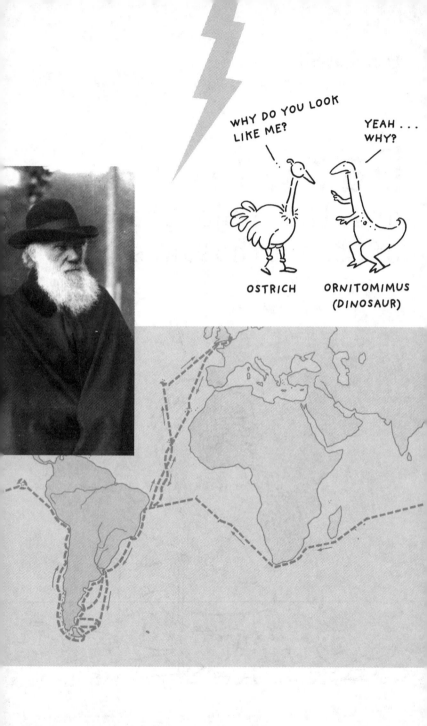

Contents

Charles Darwin

Charles Darwin was the first scientist to propose the theory of evolution, and he launched the study of the origin of man.

Though Darwin collected fossils and studied hundreds of extinct animals throughout his life, he never gave much thought to the "Dinosauria," which at that time were the favorite topic of a very small group of experts. The most significant among them were his great friend and supporter, Thomas Huxley, and his greatest opponent, Professor Richard Owen.

But the surprises don't end there. The great debate about the origin of the species had, in fact, the increasing popularity of the dinosaurs as a backdrop. Because they know a lot when it comes to evolution.

HMM . . .

WHAT YOU'LL FIND IN THIS BOOK

There's me, Charles Darwin, the narrator.

There's my voyage sailing around the world on the *Beagle*.

There's the tropical forest in the Galápagos Islands full of so many animals.

HUFF

KITTY

There's my theory of natural selection.

There are all the members of my big family and my very famous book.

There's what I think about the origin of humans.

There's also the true story of the dinosaurs.

THEY CALLED US ANTEDILUVIAN MONSTERS!

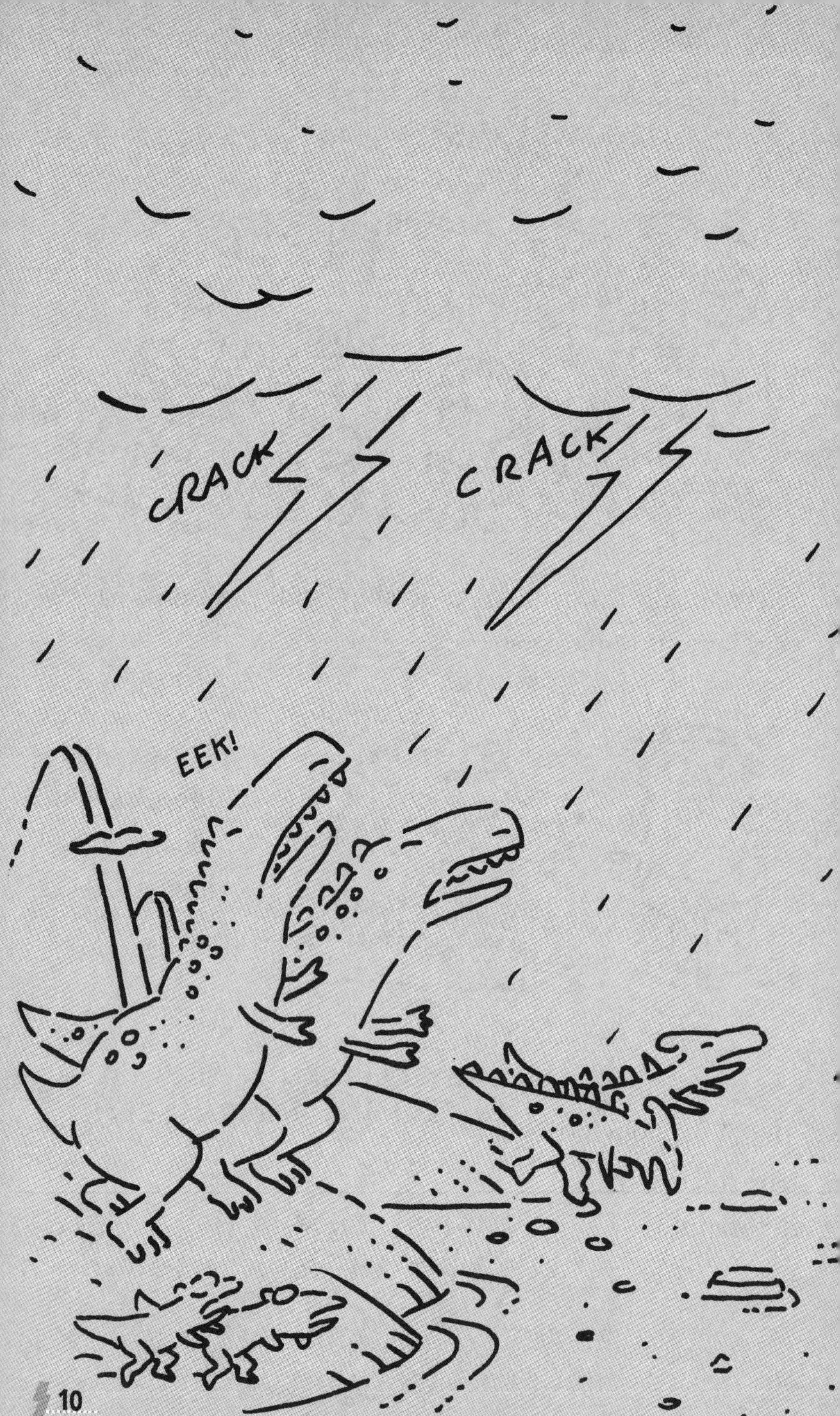
CRACK
CRACK
EEK!

Until the 17th century, most Old Word scholars were convinced that there were only a few hundred species living on Earth. The land animals, in particular, could not have been more numerous than those contained in Noah's Ark; that is, those that had been able to escape the Great Flood.

The discovery of the Americas greatly increased the number of known species.

At the same time, from the deep rocks and the dirt of the Earth, the fossil remains of a growing number of mysterious creatures were coming to light, which were thought to be gigantic monsters.

For those who believed the theory of the "book of nature," which rigidly interpreted the words of the Bible, these creatures could not have been anything other than the animals drowned in the waters of the flood. Because of this, they were called antediluvian monsters.

When Charles Darwin was born, no one knew anything about dinosaurs. To tell the truth, the word "dinosaur" did not even exist.

Of course, fossil remains of these creatures had already been found. In fact, these fossils might have given rise to the legend of the dragons—fantastic reptiles capable of breathing smoke and flames.

1. Me, Charles Darwin

Hi, everyone. I'm Charles Robert Darwin. Many people believe I'm the greatest naturalist of all time, the one who discovered natural selection, the one who removed man from the  center of creation, the one who said—though it's not completely true—that we descend from the monkey. According to my father, however, I'm only good for hunting mice.

I was born in Shrewsbury, in Shropshire, England, on February 12, 1809.

I live in Mount House, a large, three-story house with attached stables and a big meadow. It's a house for a wealthy family, and I certainly can't complain.

My mother, Susannah, died when I was eight years old.
I barely remember her: she was all embroidery and lace,
and she had many children. In fact, I have one brother and
four sisters.

My father,
Robert Waring
Darwin, is a
serious and
respected doctor.
Physically, he's big
and round: he's
almost six feet two

and weighs more than 300 pounds. He often gets angry
with me—he says that I'm not interested in anything
and that I'll disgrace myself and the whole family. He
wants me to become a doctor like him, so he talks to me
about his clinical cases, and, when he takes me on walks
through Shrewsbury, he shows me the houses where he
cared for his patients . . . or where they died.

I'm an energetic and curious little boy, but not
studious at all.

I like to go around the countryside, hunting or fishing for snails in the pond. When I can, I go horseback riding with Erasmus, my brother, or on day trips with Caroline, Susan, and Marianne, my older sisters.

I have a hobby. I collect everything I find: stamps, postmarks, but especially shells and minerals. I like to collect rocks, and I often ask myself where they really come from.

FOUND IN THE GARDEN   IN THE RIVER   ON THE BEACH

I asked myself the same question the first time I saw an "erratic boulder." It's called that because no one knows how to explain why it's there, right smack in the middle of the flat English countryside. As a matter of fact, there are mountains with the same type of rock dozens of miles away.

I'LL BE SHOCKED IF ANYONE KNOWS HOW IT GOT HERE.

In 1824 the term "Megalosaurus" (or, large reptile) appeared for the first time in a scientific paper. William Buckland, a geologist and theologian from Oxford, described in detail an animal whose fossilized bones were found and collected near the university where he taught.

The Megalosaurus is a carnivorous reptile 6 ½ feet high and 39 feet long. The antediluvian creature was incorrectly classified in the order of the saurians, or the fireflies, and was designated as such.

2. I Have an Awesome Grandpa

As little kids go, I'm quite a character. I'm pretty feisty. I often let a few bad words slip out, and I tell incredible fibs to impress the older kids.

GRANDPA ERASMUS DARWIN

I go to Reverend Butler's school. It's a big, dark, barracks-like building about a mile from my house. My scholastic performance isn't good

or bad. I find this school to be too old fashioned: we don't learn anything but ancient history and geography. What a bore!

But in the toolshed, my brother and I have made a type of chemical laboratory where I do strange experiments. The result is that they saddle me with the nickname "Gas."

POP

FIZZZ   POP

Well, I love nature a lot, and I'm not very respectful of the rules. Maybe my personality is a little like my grandpa Erasmus's. He was a super grandfather, even if my father isn't very proud of him. I never met him, because he died seven years before I was born, but at our house a lot of books and things refer to him.

To tell the truth, some of these things are a little embarrassing to a family like ours, so they try to keep them hidden from me.

I'M A REVOLUTIONARY WITH MANY WIVES AND CHILDREN!

Grandpa Erasmus was awkward, ugly, and enormously obese, and yet women were crazy about him. In fact, he had two wives, 14 kids, and an official mistress. He was also one of the most sought after doctors of his time. Even King George III invited him to London to be his personal doctor. But Grandpa Erasmus refused.

Grandpa was friends with James Watt, the inventor of the steam engine; Joseph Priestley, the great chemist; and Josiah Wedgwood (my mother's father), a noted ceramics maker. Grandpa Erasmus was also a clever inventor. He built a machine that could say "mama" and "papa," an automatic flushing toilet that worked by opening and closing the seat, and even a fake nose to cure squinting. He designed rockets, submarines, and aircraft. But the most important thing for me is that he was interested in natural sciences, and he wrote a book about evolution. That's right—Grandpa Erasmus wrote a book precisely on the topic that would become the focus of my work— and my entire existence.

LIFE ORIGINATED IN THE PRIMORDIAL SEAS!

In 1822, in the Cretaceous terrain of Sussex, England, Mrs. Mary Ann Mantell, the wife of a doctor who was passionate about paleontology, stumbled across the fossil of an enormous tooth. The fragment of what would be  dubbed Iguanodon was sent to Georges Cuvier, the greatest paleontologist of the time, who worked in Paris.

Cuvier was a master of comparative anatomy. All he needed was one bone to reconstruct an entire animal. There were many hypotheses about this creature, and the reconstructions were very far from reality. Cuvier was the only one who came close to the truth.

FISH! RHINOCEROS! HERBIVOROUS REPTILE!

DINOSAUR TOOTH

3. A Student Who "Can Do More"

Like I already said, I'm nothing special at school. Instead of staying shut up in Reverend Butler's dull school, I prefer to spend my days wandering along the river, gathering shells, and observing the flight of birds. Really, I can't understand why ornithology isn't the preferred hobby of gentlemen. I also like to walk along the seashore and stop to talk with the farmers and fishermen.

During the long winter evenings, or when I'm grounded at home, I flip through science and nature books in father's library. The one with the best pictures is Buffon's *Natural History*, which is full of designs of both familiar and exotic animals that live on various continents.

Camel
Dromedary
Alpaca
Llama
Vicuña

In the library, there are also some of Grandpa Erasmus's strange books, like the scientific poem "The Botanic Garden." The verses are in heroic couplets (sets of two rhyming lines), and it's about love and sex between plants. My grandpa—at least, this is how I see it—wrote a bunch of nonsense, but every once in a while he hit on an amazing idea. Like when he came up with the concept of DNA.

IT WOULDN'T BE THAT STRANGE IF WE DISCOVERED THAT ALL CREATURES DERIVE FROM A SINGLE LIVING FILAMENT.

But let's get back to me. So, I do little or nothing until I'm 16. Then my father enrolls me in the College of Medicine at the University of Edinburgh. I attend class there, but I'm less than enthusiastic. Then, in my third year, I have to help with a live operation. I can't bear the blood and the screams of the patient.

UUUUUGH!

ZAK SPLAT

In 1827, anesthesia still hadn't been invented, nor had lab coats, sanitation, or sterilized scalpels, for that matter. By this point, I'm sure that I'll never be a great doctor, so I abandon the operating room and leave the University of Edinburgh.

As a last-ditch effort—to quote my dad—I'm forced to enroll in the University of Cambridge.

I have a chance to earn a degree there that will allow me to obtain the sacred orders of the Church of England. Basically, I'll become an Anglican priest. A good profession, my father says.

"Dinosaur" comes from two Greek words, *deinos* and *sauros*, which mean "terrible firefly." The name was coined in 1841 by Richard Owen, an English doctor and paleontologist. A stubborn antievolutionist, and therefore bitter enemy of Darwin, Owen would always consider dinosaurs as creatures that drowned during the Great Flood—or another flood, because the notion that there had been more than one flood was gaining ground.

4. I'm an Indecisive Person

CONGRATULATIONS, MR. DARWIN

At Cambridge something unexpected happens. For the first time, my passion for nature is encouraged by two teachers: Professor John Stevens Henslow and Professor Adam Sedgwick. They also teach me how to preserve plants and insects and how to embalm birds and other animals.

I go out often with Henslow and Sedgwick to do botanical and geological investigations. They respect me, and they treat me like a friend. So, in 1831, when I'm about to take my last exams, Professor Henslow makes me an incredible offer.

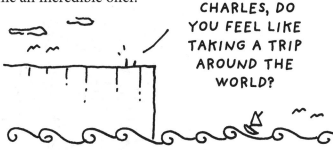

CHARLES, DO YOU FEEL LIKE TAKING A TRIP AROUND THE WORLD?

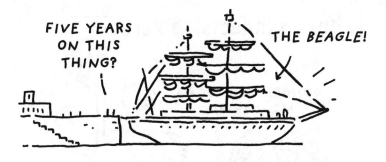

FIVE YEARS ON THIS THING?

THE BEAGLE!

The venture is very serious. It has actually been organized by the English Admiralty. The ship I would sail on belongs to His Britannic Majesty. It's a two-masted warship, and it's called the *Beagle*. Our task is to take an exploratory trip along the coasts of Peru, Chile, and Tierra del Fuego, as well as among the Pacific Islands, to create a chain of chronometric (timekeeping) stations around the world. Professor Henslow suggested that I be the naturalist on the expedition team.

Naturally, my father is furious. Not only am I not graduating in medicine, not only am I breaking family tradition and getting a useless degree, but I'm also giving up a religious career to embark on an adventure with no end in sight. He thinks I'm a good-for-nothing.

I KNEW IT! I'VE ALWAYS KNOWN IT!

So, I'll represent the University of Cambridge on this adventure. The job doesn't come with a salary. I'll be without pay for five years.

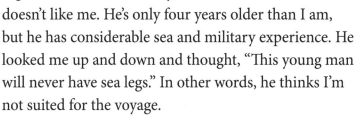

CHARLES DARWIN, I SUPPOSE

Father, however, isn't my only problem. The captain of the expedition, Robert FitzRoy, doesn't like me. He's only four years older than I am, but he has considerable sea and military experience. He looked me up and down and thought, "This young man will never have sea legs." In other words, he thinks I'm not suited for the voyage.

I, too, have some doubts. I'm used to living comfortably, and this trip on the ocean certainly won't be a walk in the park. Also—even though I don't dare confess it to Captain FitzRoy—I suffer from seasickness.

The one who calms all my fears is Uncle Jos (Josiah Wedgwood II). In fact, he argues my case to Father, who in the end gives his permission. At this point, I can no longer turn back.

LET'S HOPE FOR THE BEST

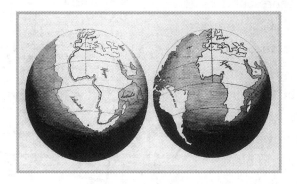

When Darwin set sail on his voyage in 1831, it was still a common belief that the Earth was only a few thousand years old. People also believed that everything on its surface—in its oceans and on its mountains—was created as it existed. No one imagined that the ocean Darwin was crossing didn't exist at one time, and that the Americas, Africa, and Asia had been united in a single continent called Pangaea, where dinosaurs and the ancestors of all animals that inhabit the Earth today once roamed.

PANGAEA!

North America
Eurasia
South America
Africa
India
Australia

5. The Adventure Begins

We set sail from Devonport on December 27, 1831. A new life begins for me today. On board the *Beagle*, I brought dozens of books, among them a Bible in Greek, Milton's *Paradise*

Lost, and a little book fresh off the press, the first volume of Charles Lyell's *Principles of Geology*. He posits a very interesting theory. He says that the great geological processes, like the rising of the mountains or the layering of the rocky strata, are not the product of floods or terrible catastrophes but are the result of the slow work of nature (still in action) over the course of millions and millions of years.

The *Beagle* is a small ship. I share my cabin with Captain FitzRoy: it is just a few square feet full of sextants and spyglasses. I have trouble finding a place for my diaries. During the trip I write dozens of them.

FitzRoy is truly unbearable. He's an aristocratic descendent (by illegitimate means) of King Charles, an official of His Majesty's Royal Fleet, and a veteran of this type of voyage. But he overreacts. He considers any answer or phrase that contradicts him as mutiny. When I dared to assert that slavery is abominable, when for him it's extremely normal, I risked having to leave the ship.

DOWN WITH SLAVERY

MR. DARWIN, HOW DARE YOU!

After the departure, I was seasick for the entire night. There were many storms for me then: in the ocean, in my stomach, and among my emotions. I'm just a beginner naturalist; in reality, I'm a candidate for the sacred order of the Church of England. Once again I asked myself,

HERE IS THE ROOM I SHARE WITH CAPTAIN FITZROY

"What am I doing here in the middle of the ocean?"

But the next morning, at dawn, when the ocean was calm, the *Beagle* slowly skirted a lush island teeming with animals and birds. Immediately, my heart and stomach became lighter. Finally, I'll set foot on dry land.

In fact, we'll disembark in Santiago, in the archipelago of Cape Verde. I'll be able to collect never-before-seen insects and flowers there. I'll finally do my job. Now I'm sure I've made the right choice, no matter how this voyage ends.

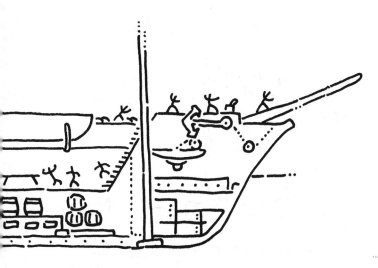

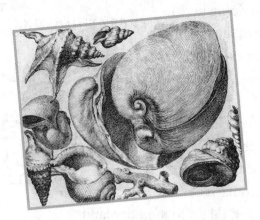

Fossils are remains, imprints, or traces of animals and plants that lived millions and millions of years ago. People have been finding them since ancient times. In China, for example, they were so common that they were called dragon bones, and they used them in medicinal potions.

To the naturalists of Darwin's era, fossils, including dinosaur remains, seemed to not have any connection to living species.

AS THOUGH WE CAME FROM ANOTHER WORLD

6. Travel Companions

On the *Beagle*, I have to live with several dozen people, including crew members, officials, and passengers. I made friends with the midshipman, Philip King, and the artist, Augustus Earle, who will immortalize with his pencil the places and creatures that we'll encounter on this voyage.

Among the others, I meet the young Syms Covington, a flute player and cabin boy who will become my assistant. He'll be very useful to me, and I'll teach him to embalm birds and preserve flowers and insects.

The *Beagle* will also transport three unusual passengers: Fuegia, York, and Jemmy. They're three Fuegians, or three inhabitants of Tierra del Fuego, the southernmost land of South America.

The three Fuegians were taken hostage by FitzRoy on a prior voyage and brought to

London. In their land they live in the nude and in freedom. In London, they were educated in the Christian faith like young Englishmen of good families. I don't see them on board very often.

But when we pass the equator, even Fuegia, York, and Jemmy appear on the

Galápagos

Brazil

Bahia

Tierra del Fuego

bridge. In fact, on ships people celebrate when they pass this imaginary line. Like all newbies, I'm blindfolded and "baptized" with seawater.

HAPPY EQUATOR, MR. CHARLES!

SPLASH!

On February 28, 1832, after two months of travel, I finally disembark on the New Continent in Bahia, Brazil. It's the first important stop on my trip around the world.

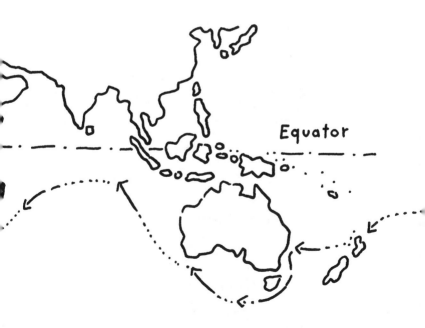

Equator

In Darwin's time, it was widely believed that species were born perfect and unchanging, created once and for all by God himself. Only the Paris-based French naturalist Jean-Baptiste, Chevalier de Lamarck (1744–1829), supported the blasphemous idea that a species could change and give rise to another. He spent many years studying invertebrates and concluded that they evolved from one another.

THE FORM
FOLLOWS THE
FUNCTION!

7. A Continent to Discover

For a naturalist, Brazil is a paradise of delights: enormous trees, vines that attach themselves to other vines, different animals, and enormous insects. You can't walk a few hundred feet without encountering a new wonder.

I found lodging on shore. Two of the midshipmen and I share a beautiful house with a yard. We're treated well here, but I certainly didn't come this far to goof off. So I leave immediately on a four-week horseback excursion. One thing I don't lack, guys, is energy!

Every day I collect hundreds of fossils, insects, and birds. Each specimen represents a new species to record. Just think, in a single day I brought home 37 different species of spiders.

But the forest also hides mysterious dangers. Eight of my *Beagle* companions went hunting, and they returned with terrible fevers, maybe from insect bites. They all died, one after the other. And it was only by chance that I didn't go hunting with them!

Anyhow, my stay in Brazil is coming to an end. I send dozens of crates of my finds to London—insects, plants, stuffed birds, and snakes preserved in alcohol.

On July 5, the *Beagle* sets sail, heading south.

According to Lamarck, one species evolves into another because it develops characteristics that are more useful for adapting to the environment in which it lives. For example, he thought that today's giraffes derived from shorter and hungrier animals whose necks elongated from one generation to the next to eat leaves from the trees of the savannah.

His theory would prove to be false. *Acquired* characteristics aren't transmitted to descendants. It would be Darwin who discovers this.

PAPA LENGTHENED HIS NECK FOR HIS WHOLE LIFE, BUT HE WON'T PASS THAT DOWN TO US EITHER

8. Welcome to Montevideo

In Montevideo a revolution is in progress. They're shooting from all sides, so it's a bad idea to leave the ship. They say that revolutions are everyday occurrences here; in one year there have actually been 10.

We go back north up the Rio de la Plata to Buenos Aires, but not everything goes smoothly here, either. In fact, an Argentine lookout greets us with cannon shots. But then they apologize, and finally we can go ashore. I'm pleasantly surprised—the women are extremely beautiful!

I see the pampas for the first time. That's what the Argentines call their endless plain. Grass, grass, and more grass as far as the eye can see.

Here I see herds of ostriches run at breakneck speed. Later I ate the eggs and meat of these animals, and I even tasted a roasted armadillo.

I found the bones of an enormous creature: a giant armadillo. These bones get me thinking . . . It's a relative of the current living species, which is a lot smaller.

We return to Montevideo. This time we're able to leave the ship. On land I have mail from England. The second volume of George Lyell's *Principles of Geology* is among the letters and packages. Lyell makes an increasingly strong case that the Earth is much older than we think. It could even be millions of years old.

But Captain FitzRoy is convinced that the Earth is a few thousand years old at most, and many people agree with him.

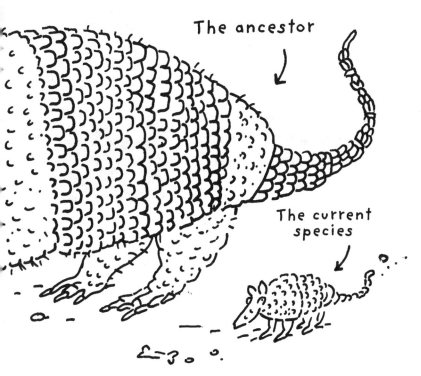

The ancestor

The current species

Although incorrect, Lamarck's theory was revolutionary: the species weren't created perfect and unchanging.

Around the same time, another scientist, the English geologist Charles Lyell, threw the sacred truths into crisis after studying Earth's volcanoes and glaciers. He also went to Sicily to study Mount Etna. He proved that volcanic mountains are formed through the slow accumulation of lava flow and not from a single eruption. The earth is therefore much older than what was described in the Bible, and its current appearance is the result of long, slow changes. This idea would have a great influence on Darwin.

9. Tierra del Fuego

The *Beagle* leaves Montevideo and Buenos Aires behind, and it heads toward Tierra del Fuego. Farther south there is only Antarctica. It's called Tierra del Fuego because, when Magellan visited it for the first time, its coasts were illuminated with countless bonfires that had been lit by its inhabitants, the Ona and the Yahgan.

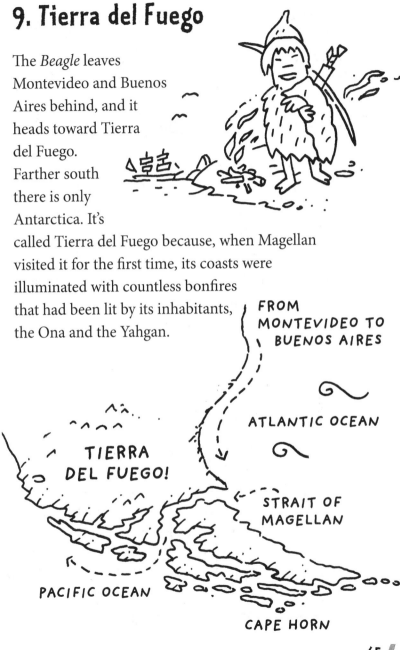

FROM MONTEVIDEO TO BUENOS AIRES

ATLANTIC OCEAN

TIERRA DEL FUEGO!

STRAIT OF MAGELLAN

PACIFIC OCEAN

CAPE HORN

When I met these populations, I was disconcerted. They're extremely poor and lack modern advancements. I didn't think that humans were capable of surviving in these conditions: The Ona sleep in the nude even in freezing temperatures. They barely cover themselves with animal skins, and they protect themselves from the cold by smearing fat on their bodies.

They live by hunting and fishing, eating mollusks, and migrating from one place to another when the food runs out. How do they do it?

We look for a place to establish a small colony. That's where we leave Fuegia, York, and Jemmy, the three Fuegians educated in London. They depart together with a missionary, bringing some goods with them that they consider indispensible: cabbage seeds, linen clothing, and porcelain teapots.

I have the suspicion that they weren't happy in London.

The missionary gives up, and when we come back we'll find the three young Fuegians dressed in furs and covered in fat, once again in a daily struggle to survive, on the perpetual hunt for food and shelter. And yet—and this is upsetting to me— none of them will express the desire to return to London and to what we call civilization.

Darwin did not find traces of dinosaurs on his voyage, but he did find fossils of many other extinct species. It was becoming clear to him that there was a close relationship between these and the living species.

But why, he asked himself, did one find fossils of so many extinct species? And how did the new ones form? This fossil cranium was collected by Darwin in Argentina. It belonged to a Toxodon. This extinct animal was a rodent the size of an elephant, and it lived in the water, a strange middle ground between a rat and a hippopotamus.

10. Nature Lessons

In South America, I learned so many things. On the Falkland Islands—or Malvinas, as the Argentines call them—I found mountains of fossil shells, witnesses to extremely long ago eras. I studied the life of the guanacos, which the gauchos captured with bolas. I discovered that where I now find many fossils of extinct animals, the landscape once wasn't a forest but was a savannah.

With the native people I visited the current forests, which are infested with jaguars, the true and proper tigers of South America.

I also subjected myself to incredible hardships. For example, I rode 400 miles (650 km) in 12 days. Under the leadership of Captain FitzRoy, we went upstream in a river for 225 miles (370 km). We often had to drag the boats ourselves by tying them to our bodies and walking along the shore.

I suffered hunger and thirst, but I was truly happy.

I often had to protect my body and face from mosquitoes and other insects. In places where I had to work without gloves, I saw my hands turn black from the large swarms of insects, which quickly got busy sucking my blood. I even had a fever for three days, but I hope it's nothing serious.

I discovered something incredible: the land here raised itself 6,500 feet (2,000 m) above sea level!

SHELLS HERE TOO!

It is not easy to find dinosaur fossils. They are buried under layers and layers of rock and sediment. Today we know that the Earth's crust is like a layer cake. Every stratum (layer) captures a period in the history of our planet. The deepest strata correspond to the older periods. Sometimes where there were seas there are now mountains, plains, and rivers. And vice versa.

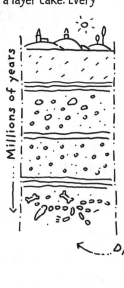

Millions of years

← Dinosaurs

11. The Islands of Diversity

Now we're in the Pacific Ocean. We've crossed the Strait of Magellan and sailed along the coasts of Chile and Peru. And in the city of Conception, I witnessed a change in the Earth's crust. Because of a strong earthquake, the terrain is visibly raised with respect to the sea level.

Along the coast, I took samples with a "blue pigeon," a hollow piece of lead that is dragged along the bottom of the ocean to collect specimens. At this point, I guess how the coral reefs were formed: in shallow seas, the coral grow continuously, adding themselves to the remains of other coral.

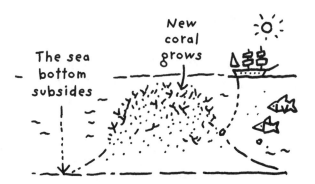

The sea bottom subsides

New coral grows

On September 15, 1835, I'm in the Galápagos, an archipelago 500 miles (800 km) from the Peruvian coast. They're peculiar islands; they are all near the equator but each is different in climate, temperature, and vegetation.

Their fauna (animal life) makes something clear to me.

For example, think about the giant tortoise. When we look at the shape and color of its shell, we can figure out which island it comes from. In fact, every island has its own species of tortoise, finch, and iguana, similar yet diverse from those of the mainland.

It seems that every island has "produced" the species most adapted to its environment.

WHAT'S YOUR SPECIALTY?

GALÁPAGOS

MAINLAND

B C D

55

During the stop in the Galápagos, Darwin observed (among other things) that 13 species of finch lived on these very distant islands, and they were similar to one another and to the species living on the mainland. There was a noticeable difference, however, in the shape of their beaks. Darwin thought that this was no accident.

More than likely, a single species of finch had arrived on the islands thousands of years before, which had then given rise to the 13 different species. The different islands of the Galápagos offered a great variety of foods and places to nest to the first species of finch, which, not being threatened by rival species, began to adapt differently according to the particular environmental conditions in which they found themselves.

12. The Voyage Around the World

We stayed in the Galápagos for six weeks. Then we steered toward Tahiti, a very beautiful island inhabited by delightful indigenous peoples.

Then we reach New Zealand, where we celebrate the Christmas of 1835 among the Maori.

Finally, on January 12, 1836, we disembarked in Australia.

For a naturalist, this continent is another world. It's as though it were made by a different creator. It's populated by incredible animals: there are creatures that look like a cross between mammals and birds, kangaroos, and even wolves with pouches.

It almost seems like this land that is so far away from us has produced the most distant and diverse species from all those we know.

We finally return to the sea. We cross the Indian Ocean, skirt the Mauritius Islands and Madagascar, sail around the Cape of Good Hope, see the island of Saint Helena, and, finally, after a forced stop in Bahia, head toward England.

Unfortunately, I'm sick. I'm getting feverish more often. For this reason I'm happy to return home.

After almost five years of travel, the *Beagle* sights the port of Falmouth.

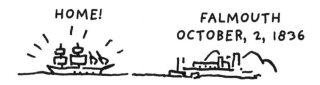

HOME!

FALMOUTH
OCTOBER, 2, 1836

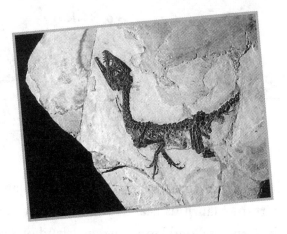

Today we know that the dinosaurs appeared on Earth 228 million years ago. They populated it for more than 160 million years. During this extremely long period, they diversified into about 700 species: herbivores, carnivores, marine, and terrestrial. Some reached 100 feet (30 m) in length. But there were also dinosaurs as small as a mouse.

13. A Successful Naturalist

My father says that after my voyage on the *Beagle* my head has gotten big. I think that it actually has; at least on the inside, something has changed for sure.

I have a lot to do—I have to organize the finds that I sent to England. It's a good thing that Professor Owen is giving me a hand.

I have also become famous. Some animals specimens I sent from the *Beagle* intrigued even the nonprofessionals. So I've been invited to the best salons in London. Women and young ladies crowd around me

to ask me about the faraway countries that I visited. Between you and me, this interest pleases me greatly.

EMMA

But I'm not cut out for the hectic life of the city. I would like a wife, some kids, and a house in the country. So, on November 11, 1838, I ask Emma Wedgwood, my dear and beautiful cousin, to marry me. She accepts.

Together we move to Down House, a large villa with a garden, greenhouse, and stable.

In December 1839, William, the first of my 10 children, is born.

WAAAH!

In 1839 I also publish my first book, which recounts my voyage around the world. It's basically my diary from my time on the *Beagle*.

I speak and write about geology. I confirm that Lyell was right: the environment and the Earth's crust have not always been the way they are, and that's not because of repeated and catastrophic global floods. Instead, it is the result of the action of forces still in progress, capable of raising and engulfing marine floors until they become mountains as high as 6,500 feet (2,000 m), or trenches just as deep, in a very slow and incessant change.

At the beginning of the dinosaur era, when the exposed
lands constituted a single, large continent, some strange
creatures were common. They were part reptile and part
mammal. One of these was Cynognathus, a term that means
"dog jaw." It was probably covered in fur. It is an ancestor of
the mammals and is therefore also one of our ancestors.

HE STILL HASN'T DECIDED
WHAT HE WANTS TO
DO WHEN HE
GROWS UP.

CYNOGNATHUS

14. The Origin of Species

I speak and write eagerly about my voyage around the world, but I only have the courage to confess to a few friends the disturbing idea that it produced in my mind: I believe, in fact, that over time the species can change, and that they do change. For you, perhaps, this idea doesn't  seem strange, but for my fellow scientists it means calling into question the perfect work of God. Without concrete proof, I don't want to open my mouth.

Also, I still haven't been able to understand the mechanism by which species are formed. But it becomes clear when, in 1838, I read a book by Thomas Robert Malthus. The book causes a sensation. It's entitled *An Essay on the Principle of Population*.

Malthus says revolutionary things—for example, that when there isn't enough food for everyone, only the strongest survive, while the weak die. It's certainly not fair, but now I'm able to clearly see the mechanism that leads from one species to another: the species evolve through natural selection.

THE STRUGGLE FOR EXISTENCE

ACCORDING TO ROBERT MALTHUS

When the environmental conditions change, those who have the most favorable characteristics for living in the new conditions survive. Then they reproduce and transmit those characteristics to their offspring.

Try to think of the original species of giraffe. There were giraffes with short necks, others with medium necks, and still others with long necks. They all used to nibble grass. But only those with the long necks could also eat the leaves of the higher trees.

Then the environmental conditions changed. The grass disappeared, and the tree leaves were all that remained as food. Then only the long-necked giraffes survived . . . the current species.

WHAT A HISTORY!

Professor Owen, the father of the dinosaurs and the director of the British Museum, came up with the idea to build some dinosaur models and exhibit them to the public. Under his direction and with the help of the painter and sculptor Richard Hawkins, a shipyard was used to assemble the gigantic antediluvians. They were exhibited in 1851 at the Crystal Palace in London.

The exhibit was an enormous success. Although spectacular, Owen's reconstructions were quite wrong. The assembly of a prehistoric animal is not a simple undertaking, not even today.

15. I Have to Enter the Field

By now I'm confident in my theory of natural selection, but I still don't reveal it. I write a draft, I develop it into an essay, but I don't publish anything. Instead, I withdraw into a shell, so to speak, to study some strange creatures: the cirripeds, a species of

crustacean that seems infinitely varied. It's a worthwhile study: it confirms that the cirriped is a variety that natural selection acts on. In other words, I try to support my simple theory with a mountain of proof and conclusive arguments.

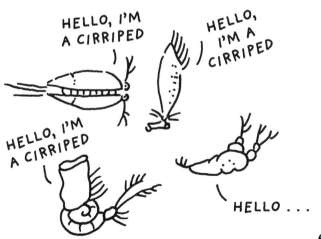

But then, unexpectedly, in 1856 Alfred Russel Wallace sends me a short essay from Borneo. Wallace is a naturalist colleague who, after years of observations, expresses opinions very similar to mine.

I can't stay silent any longer. In July 1858, at the Linnean Society, mutual friends organize the reading of two scientific papers: one mine, the other Wallace's. The theory of evolution by natural selection becomes public.

I put aside the mountain of papers that is becoming my "great book" and develop an extract of a few pages titled *The Origin of Species*.

And then an incredible thing happens: the 1,250 copies of the first edition sell out in a day. Then the second edition sells like hotcakes, and so does the third. Almost everyone likes my theory, even the public at large. But Professor Owen doesn't like it at all.

When Professor Owen coined the name "dinosaur," Thomas Huxley, a doctor and naturalist, as well as a close friend of Darwin and supporter of the notion of evolution, proposes another: "ornithoscelid." The term highlights the similarities between dinosaurs and birds, but Owen dismisses it with scorn.

DINOSAURS AND BIRDS ... WHAT HAVE THEY GOT TO DO WITH IT?

16. An Impeccable Theory

My little book is reviewed in *Time* by Thomas Huxley, who describes my idea as a type of "egg of Columbus." Thomas is a dear friend on top of being the most brilliant English zoologist. He supports me, along with many other scholars and even clergy, such as Charles Kingsley, a priest and a novelist.

NAILED IT

THOMAS HENRY HUXLEY

But there are also people like Father Philip Gosse, who wrote an entire book to discredit me. In it he says that the world was created in six days: Adam and Eve with their perfectly formed belly buttons, all the living species, and the rocks with fossils already inside.

Adam

Eve

Rocks with dinosaur fossils?

In fact, since it seems that I have questioned the theory of divine creation recounted in the Bible, someone calls me "the most dangerous man in England."

But my worst enemy is certainly Professor Richard Owen, the father of the dinosaurs. He's a distinguished paleontologist, but he's also nasty and rather envious. He provides information and support to Bishop Wilberforce, my adversary in what would become one of the most famous debates of Oxford.

Luckily, my friend Huxley always has a prompt reply!

Abroad, things are going better. In Germany, Ernst Haeckel, the inventor of the word *ecology*, supports me. In the United States, despite the fact that there are so many religious fundamentalists, all the young people are on my side. Only in France is there some opposition. I may be too attached to the ideas of Cuvier and Lamarck, but ultimately everyone agrees with the soundness of my theory.

In 1858, a dinosaur was found that had front limbs very similar to wings: the *Compsognathus longpipes*. This dinosaur walked upright and could fly short distances, like hens. It was a true link between dinosaurs and birds, a confirmation of Darwin's theory of evolution. But for the creationists, such as Professor Owen, Compsognathus was a fraud, created precisely to support the claims of the evolutionists.

17. The Descent of Man

My life is now forever tied to the debate about evolution. These are hard times, and I become the subject of very aggressive attacks, especially when I expand on my theory of evolution to include humans when I publish the book *The Descent of Man* in 1871.

VOILÀ

"Man descends from the monkey," the newspaper headlines read, even though I never said that. Cartoons and satirical articles pour forth.

At a university where I'm holding a conference, a real, live baby monkey with the sign MISSING LINK is even lowered into the classroom.

SIR CHARLES DARWIN

HA! HA!

Anyway, my book on the theory of man is a success, as is its sequel that I publish the year after: *The Expression of the Emotions in Man and Animals*.

In it I often make amusing comparisons. Humans, I say, bear in their bodily frames the permanent stamp of their kinship and their lowly origin.

Thomas Huxley was the first to support an evolutionary link between dinosaurs and birds (1863). In the years that followed, many other fossils were discovered that demonstrate this relationship.

Today there are even those who think that we should separate the dinosaurs into two groups: "non-avian dinosaurs" and "avian dinosaurs."

Nevertheless, the result is the same: the dinosaurs evolved according to the rules of natural selection defined by Darwin. They became birds and are, among the vertebrates, the most diverse groups after mammals.

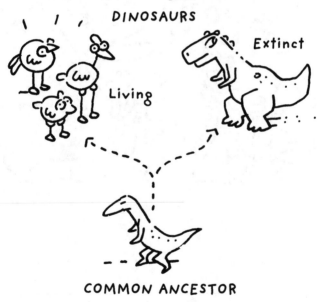

DINOSAURS

Extinct

Living

COMMON ANCESTOR

18. Living with Nature

These are the last years of my life. I live in Down House. In the greenhouse I grow orchids—I study how they're pollinated by insects and how these insects influence evolution.

My garden is full of pigeons, and I joined two breeding clubs. I'm able to demonstrate how humans' actions influence the varieties of a species they breed.

EARTHWORM

In the garden there is also a "wormstone." I use it to demonstrate that earthworms are capable of burying entire buildings and cities with their work.

I also study my children and their behavior. My studies will be the foundation of modern anthropology.

WHAT PATIENCE!

I become very popular, especially among the progressives. But when Karl Marx offers to dedicate his book to me, I politely decline the offer. It doesn't seem right. He and I talk about different things.

Das Kapital

Unfortunately, my fevers and the seizures, left over from my voyage so many years before, are becoming more frequent. In other words, my time is about to end. I'm calm, and my heart is at peace.

BRRR!

BRRR!

Charles Darwin died on April 19, 1882, in Down House, probably due to an illness contracted years before in South America.

He never intended to overturn the ideas about the world. And yet he did just that. Just as Copernicus took Earth from the center of the universe, Darwin took man from the center of creation.

Today this might not seem so revolutionary, but we live the consequences of it every day: humans are now responsible for their role in nature.

Many books and images represent Darwin as a great old man who was ill and had a long beard, with a wise and serious air about him.

But he was also once young, bold, and funny. He was a democrat and an abolitionist. Today he would certainly be here with us to talk about dinosaurs and ecology.

Ten Questions for Dr. Charles Darwin

A Special Interview on a Special Occasion

The occasion was Darwin Day on February 12, 2009, the 200th birthday of the great naturalist, an anniversary celebrated by scientific institutions around the world.

The interview was conducted by Luca Novelli, who was not new to these endeavors. In preparation for the event, he went to London's Westminster Cathedral and asked to meet with Dr. Charles Darwin in person. The location—formal and a bit dark—wasn't suitable for a relaxed meeting. So, the interviewee and the interviewer went outside and sat at a table at the nearest diner. Questions and answers proceeded as follows.

Dr. Darwin, forgive me for interrupting your eternal peace, but your ideas are again creating a big stir. There are those who say that your theory actually contains some errors. Would you have expected this on your 200th birthday?

No trouble at all, Mr. Novelli. First of all, thank you for giving me a reason to come out for a breath of fresh air. It takes me back to the evenings in Cambridge, in the company of my university friends, when I still didn't know what I was going to do with my life.

Anyhow, with respect to what you're asking me, I'm embarrassed. My theory contains errors and omissions? It could be; it's only a scientific theory. But evolution by natural selection is still the most reasonable response to the question, How are living species born?

All scientific theories allow for corrections and exceptions. Today you know about DNA, genetics, and the origin of mutations on which natural selection operates. These are things that not even I imagined, but that determine how and where evolution occurs. I thank all those who have followed in my footsteps and who are continuing my work. I consider their contributions to be the best birthday gifts.

There are those who say that you inspired ideas that con-flict with human rights. And there are even those who still suggest that your theory of evolution by natural selection is contrary to religion. Are they right?

My friend Thomas Huxley would describe them as shameful conjectures. I never wanted to enter into the merits of the eternal conflict between Good and Evil with my theory. Nor did I want to put a limit on the rights and opportunities that every individual on this Earth must have. These are civil rights that I have strenuously defended.

Evolution describes only what happened over the course of millions of years to living species, including our own. Between you and me, we're here because our ancestors were more suited to surviving than their contemporaries. But applying my theory to social and political thought is risky, and I don't agree with doing that. I didn't do it in life, and I don't do it now.

Finally, with respect to religion . . . well, I'm astonished that in your time there are still arguments about this topic. I was a man of faith, and I was even about to become a pastor of the Church of England. For those who believe in God, nothing changes if someone demonstrates that Creation occurred over 15 billion years instead of 7 days. Time is relative, as Einstein said. In our universe, one day could be equal to a million years in another. It seems naïve that this couldn't also be true for the Bible, which contains wonderful stories full of meaning, like that of Noah's Ark, which isn't to be taken literally.

Dr. Darwin, have you ever considered the possibility that there might have really been a Great Flood?

The flood was Captain Robert FitzRoy's obsession. During the *Beagle*'s voyage, every time we found the bones of some large, extinct animal, FitzRoy would say, "Here's another antediluvian creature." During our voyage around the world, we found evidence of many catastrophes that had certainly led to large-scale extinctions of animals and plants. But this must not make us lose sight of the process of creation of new species, which is gradual and so slow that it could last millions of years.

When did you begin to understand how evolution functions?

Definitely during my voyage around the world. It wasn't only a great adventure but a mental journey that helped me to understand natural selection and to sense many other connected natural phenomena.

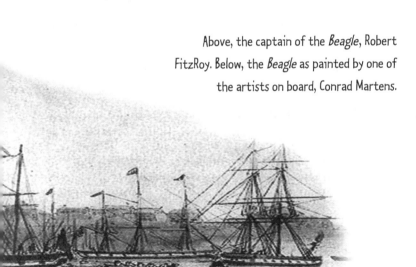

Above, the captain of the *Beagle*, Robert FitzRoy. Below, the *Beagle* as painted by one of the artists on board, Conrad Martens.

One of the criticisms of your theory is the fact that one doesn't always find fossils of the intermediary creatures between the present-day species and the antediluvian ones. How do you explain this absence of missing links?

Capybara

Mr. Novelli, certain people who write nonsense about me should load a backpack on their shoulders and repeat the voyage I took before opening their mouths. They would quickly see how evolution occurs in nature—so simply, instant after instant, over the course of millions of years.

Today we know only a small part of the species that live on our planet, and there are more than one and a half million. Many more are extinct, and while they were evolving or becoming extinct, the Earth's crust was turned inside out, squeezed, and shaken like a carpet many times. So, very few traces of past species remain.

But just by looking at the present-day species you can get an idea of the infinite variations that a life form can take over the course of evolution. For example, the ancestors of whales were as small as mice and ran on dry land. A little at a time, over hundreds of thousands of years, they increasingly adapted to the ocean environment. We have few fossils of the intermediary forms, but by touring the world we can find so many similar species . . . to the missing links.

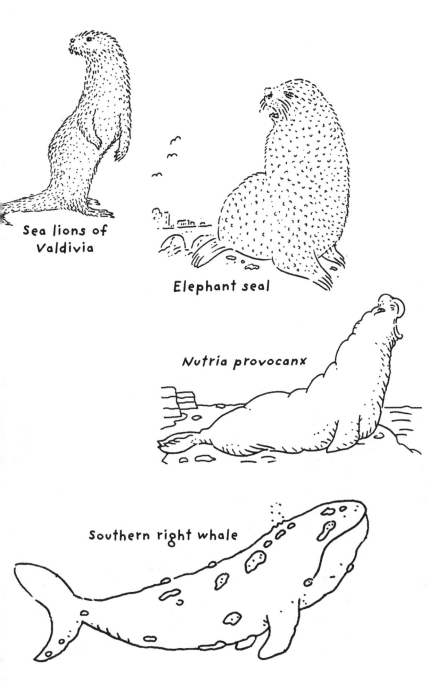

Sea lions of
Valdivia

Elephant seal

Nutria provocanx

Southern right whale

Still, those who want to attack your theory emphasize that at its core is the struggle for survival and the supremacy of the fittest. This point is, actually, rather negative.

To start, I never talked about the supremacy of the fittest—of the best adapted, if anything. Take, for example, the marine iguanas that live on the Galápagos. When their ancestors arrived on these volcanic islands, there was little to eat on the dry land. Only those that adapted to swimming underwater and eating marine algae survived, not the strong and domineering ones. That's how a new species is born.

With regard to humans, then, the brain is the organ that has evolved most over the course of the last 100,000 years. At the more difficult times, it was the most intelligent

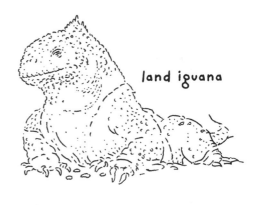

land iguana

who survived, not the biggest or strongest. If supremacy of the fittest were valid, physically we would all resemble Arnold Schwarzenegger. Instead, we see a certain amount of variety around us . . . even in brains.

Below, the marine iguana on a Galápagos beach

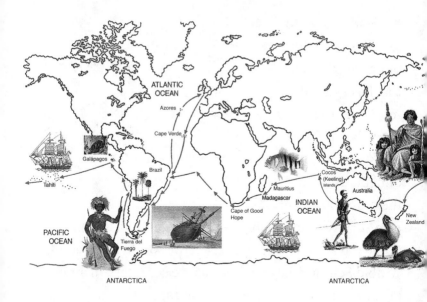

It really seems like it was one of the most important events of your career as a scientist. Is this true?

Definitely, yes. But the journey on board the *Beagle* wasn't the most interesting part. I suffered from seasickness, and as soon as I could I headed to shore. For example, I stayed in Rio de Janeiro for several months while the *Beagle* did some surveying on the coast of Brazil. Also, I was hosted by friends in Buenos Aires, where I arrived on horseback after crossing 375 miles of the pampas. While in Buenos Aires, the *Beagle* never docked; it was an English war ship, and it would have been blasted with cannon shots from the Argentine capital.

I also stayed on land for a long time in Chile, Tahiti, and Australia. In fact, it was on land that I did the major part of my observations and deductions. In this way I saw extremely diverse environments, from the tropical forests to the Patagonian steppe, to the immense glaciers that emerge from the sea, to active volcanoes. These landscapes made me understand that the Earth's crust is constantly moving, and that environments change slowly and inexorably. The creatures that populate them adapt to these environments to form new species, or they become extinct.

Turtles of Santa Cruz, one of the islands of the archipelago of the Galápagos

Dr. Darwin, after circumnavigating the southern hemisphere, didn't you ever wish to visit other regions of our planet?

I contracted a serious illness during the voyage of the *Beagle* that later prevented me from leading a healthy and normal life. I suffered from recurring fevers and sudden pain, so I retired to Down House. I lived and worked there with my wife and children for the rest of my days.

I would have liked to have visited the Alps and their glaciers. There, too, like in the Andes, you can find marine fossils at high altitudes. I know that at one time the Dolomites were coral atolls right in the middle of a tropical sea. I would have liked to climb them. Even in

the rest of Europe I would have found interesting fossils. Where Paris is now, large, furry rhinoceroses once grazed, and in the Po Valley whales and dolphins swam. I'm a little sorry that I couldn't go on excursions to these places too. If you get the chance, please do it for me as well . . .

Above, the peak in the Andes that was named after Captain FitzRoy, in Patagonia. Below, Magellanic penguins photographed in Tierra del Fuego.

What do you like and dislike about the world today?

I'm fairly up to date. I can't help but listen to the whirl of human thoughts that fill Westminster Cathedral every day. I must say that you've made a lot of progress. You've defeated terrible illnesses, you no longer use horse-drawn carriages, you no longer fear famine, you travel in a moment from New York to Singapore . . . but you're distracted and somewhat worried about the human species. You have profoundly changed the natural environment, and you're changing the planet's climate with unpredictable results. It almost seems like you never stop for a moment to think. In my century, times were different. Before publishing my theory, I hemmed and hawed for 20 years. . . . Instead, you do so many things, and all so fast. I even fear that in London my countrymen no longer have time to stop and take tea at five o' clock in the afternoon. It's terrible.

What do you advise us to do?

Live more in nature and incorporate more nature into your lives. I advise you to stop and reflect a hundred times before destroying a landscape, a forest, or a single plant. Get back to human biological rhythms without trying to compete with those of your machines, your computers, and your robots . . . which are at your service and not vice versa.

My hope is that humanity evolves its civilization toward lifestyles that are more sustainable for the planet. More moderate lifestyles can be sources of more happiness and health than the current ones. This is also my wish.

Happy evolution to everyone!

A Darwinian Dictionary

AND . . . LIKE EVOLUTION

ADAM AND EVE

According to Darwin, the human species did not originate from a single Adam and a single Eve, but through evolution from a prior species. This occurred through natural selection of a pre-human species of many thousands of individuals.

ANTHROPOLOGY

The branch of science that studies human life in its various aspects.

HOMO SAPIENS
21ST CENTURY

ARCHAEOPTERYX

A dinosaur with feathers and other characteristics typical of birds. It is considered a link between birds and dinosaurs.

AS A DINOSAUR I FEEL STRANGE

BOLAS

Used by the gauchos of the Argentine pampas to capture ostriches and guanacos. They are made with two stones that are wrapped in leather and tied together by a leather cord.

BUFFON, GEORGES LOUIS LECLERC (1707–1788)

French naturalist who wrote the monumental and richly illustrated *Natural History*, which was the first work to present the similarities and relationships between species that were distant geographically but close biologically.

CATASTROPHISM, THEORY OF

Theory that proposes the Earth is cyclically subject to terrible catastrophes. It was very in vogue in the 19th century when a single global flood was no longer enough to explain the history of the Earth and the origin of the fossils that came to light. Cuvier, Owen, and other anti-evolutionists hypothesized that many global floods had followed. In reality, Earth was cyclically the object of terrible extinctions, caused according to some by the impact of immense meteorites.

IT MUST BE THE METEORITE THAT ENDED THE JURASSIC PERIOD.

CATASTROPHISTS

Supporters of the theory of catastrophism. In the early 19th century, Cuvier, Owen, and many other anti-evolutionists supported the idea of repeated great floods and repeated creations.

COMPARATIVE ANATOMY

The field of studying the anatomy of various animals, comparing their organs, and establishing where they are similar. In that way, the shape and the functions of the organs of the entire animal can be determined from a few fossil fragments.

CONTINENTAL DRIFT

Theory according to which the continents float on the Earth's crust. When dinosaurs first roamed the planet there was a single continent: Pangaea. It then fragmented into various pieces: the Americas, Eurasia, Australia, India. . . . Over the course of millions of years these pieces moved on the crust, giving rise to continuous climatic and environmental changes.

CORAL

Marine animal (Coelenterata: Anthozoa) similar to a flowering plant. Its skeletons formed the atolls and coral reefs of the Pacific Ocean. Similar formations, reemerging and rising to sea level, have become mountains, like the Dolomites.

CREATIONISTS

Supporters of the fixedness of the species, created from time to time through divine or supernatural intervention.

CUVIER, GEORGES
(1769–1832)

French naturalist, founder of paleontology, and expert on comparative anatomy. For his entire life he was a staunch creationist and catastrophist.

DARWIN, ERASMUS (1731–1802)

Friendly grandfather of Charles Darwin. A diverse and curious scholar, he anticipated some concepts later developed by his grandson and even the idea of DNA.

DNA

An important molecule contained in all the living cells, component of the genes, and on which is written "the blueprint" of the entire individual.

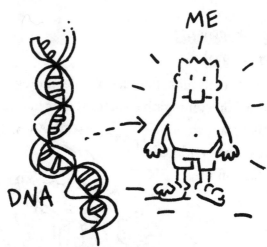

ME

DNA

EARLE, AUGUSTUS

Darwin's travel companion and the first artist who illustrated the *Beagle*'s adventure around the world. In those days, photography had not yet been invented, and his drawings are the only visual documents of the trip that we have today. Here is the *Beagle* under repair on the banks of the Rio Santa Cruz in Patagonia.

EARTHWORMS

Worms that live in the earth and ingest soil to extract the nutrients they need. They contribute to the enrichment and mixing of the soil. Darwin demonstrated that they are able to bury houses, entire towns . . . and even Stonehenge.

ERRATIC BOULDERS

In certain areas, they were called "devil's masses" because of the impossibility of explaining their presence and origin. In the majority of cases, they are found on the beds of ancient glaciers that have melted. A river of ice brought them to their location.

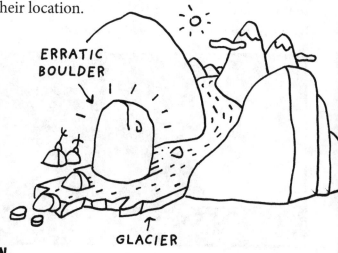

ERRATIC BOULDER

GLACIER

EVOLUTION

A process that leads from one species to another through natural selection. It began millions and millions of years ago and continues today.

IT CONTINUES

FLOOD

The one described in the Bible killed all the animals except for the hundred or so saved by Noah.

FOSSILS

Remains, imprints, or traces of animals or plants that lived in the past, some millions and millions of years ago.

GALÁPAGOS

A group of islands of volcanic origin in the Pacific Ocean. They straddle the equator but are surrounded by a cold current. For Darwin, the animal species here clarified the effects of isolation and the mechanisms by which natural selection operates.

GALÁPAGOS ISLANDS

GENE

A segment of DNA, which contains a hereditary characteristic.

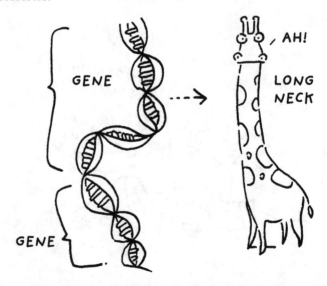

GENE

GENE

, AH!

LONG NECK

GENETIC MUTATIONS

Random changes (through radiation or otherwise) of DNA. They can be useless, dangerous, or useful. They contribute to the variability of the species on which natural selection operates.

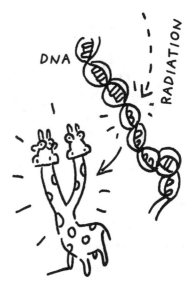

GENETICS

Science that studies hereditary characteristics and how they're passed on from parents to their offspring.

FELIX

DOMESTICA   LEO   TIGRIS

GENUS

Systematic grouping of various related species. The living species belonging to the same genus have evident ancestors in common.

GEOLOGICAL ERAS

Long units of time into which the history of Earth is divided (Archeozoic, Mesozoic, Neozoic). In turn, the eras are divided into periods. The Mesozoic Era is divided into the Triassic, Jurassic, and Cretaceous periods.

TRIASSIC   JURASSIC   CRETACEOUS   WE ARE HERE

230   208   136   65

← - - - · · · MILLIONS OF YEARS

GEOLOGY

Science that studies the history of earth and the formation of rocks and minerals.

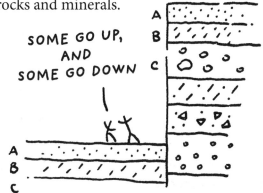

GUANACO

Similar to the llama, a relative of camels, it lives in the Andes. Unfortunately for the guanaco, it has a very soft and valuable fur coat.

HEREDITARY CHARACTERISTICS

Physical characteristics that are passed from parents to children; for example, hair and eye color, skin color, and height. Some can be favorable in certain environmental conditions, others in different conditions.

LAMARCK, JEAN BAPTISTE (1744–1829)

French naturalist who supported the idea that acquired characteristics can be inherited. His theory proved false. Only genetic mutations are hereditary.

LINNAEUS

FELIX DOMESTICA

FELIX LEO

HOMO SAPIENS

LINNAEUS, OR CARL VON LINNÉ (1707-1778)

Swedish naturalist who invented the binomial (two-name: genus and species) system of classification of animals and plants.

LYELL, CHARLES (1797-1875)

English naturalist, father of modern geology.

THE EARTH CHANGES SLOWLY!

MENDEL, GREGOR (1822–1884)

Slovakian naturalist and monk who came up with
the laws that regulate the transmission of hereditary
characteristics. His work remained unknown until the
beginning of the 20th century.

I DISCOVERED THEM
CROSS-FERTILIZING
PEA PLANTS

MISSING LINK

Evolution can be represented by a chain composed of
many species. Darwin's opponents claimed that his
theory was false because fossils of intermediate species
hadn't been found.

NOT
FOUND

MONKEY

Man does not descend from the monkey, just as we cannot descend from one of our cousins. However, *Homo sapiens* and apes have extinct common ancestors.

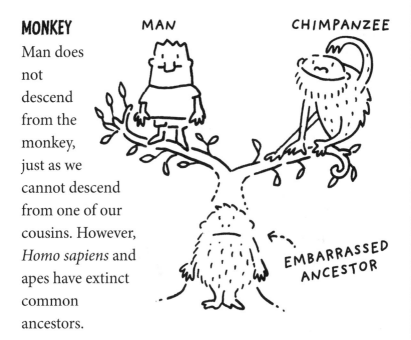

PALEONTOLOGY

Field that involves the study of fossils, their identification, and how they are dated.

SPECIES

One or more populations of individuals capable of mating and bearing fertile offspring.

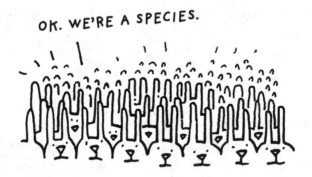

OK. WE'RE A SPECIES.

THEORY OF THE ATOLLS

Darwin's theory about the formation of the atolls and the coral reefs. Mountains sink, and the corals grow upon their own skeletons, becoming emerged land.

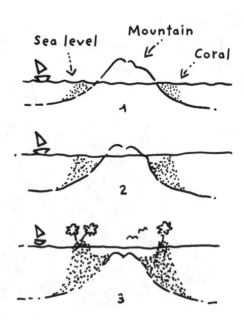

TOXODON

A large mammal from South America that has been extinct for some time. It was studied by Charles Darwin. It was as large as an elephant, and it had rodent teeth.

TREE

Evolution can be represented as a tree with many forked branches. The trunk and the large branches contain the common ancestors.

VARIABILITY

Distribution of the differences within a population or a species. Natural selection favors the "differences" more suited to the survival of the species.

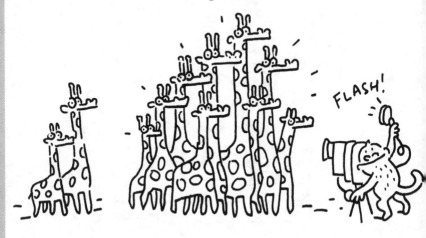

VARIETY

Small group within a species that differs in some minor characteristics.

LUCA NOVELLI

Writer, artist, journalist. He is the author of books about science and nature that have been translated across the world. He has collaborated with the Italian television company, Rai, with WWF, and with museums and universities. He wrote and directed the *Lampi di Genio in TV* (*Flashes of Genius on TV*) show for Rai Educational (www.lampidigenio.it).

He won the Legambiente (League for the Environment) award in 2001 and the Andersen Prize for popularizing science in 2004.

FLASHES OF GENIUS

A series of biographies of the great scientists—all written and illustrated by Luca Novelli—told in the voice of the protagonist. It is a fun and engaging way to approach science and to get to know the great masters that changed the history of mankind. The series won the Legambiente award in 2004.

FLASHES / OF GENIUS

Einstein
and the Time Machine

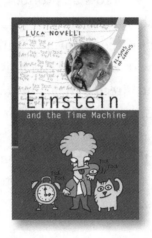

Albert Einstein wasn't afraid to think for himself. Working as a clerk in the patent office in Bern, Switzerland, he wrote papers with fantastical theories—that light is both a wave and a particle; that matter can become energy, and energy can become matter; that space can "bend," and time is relative. His revolutionary theories turned the world of physics upside down, and earned him a Nobel Prize. *Einstein and the Time Machine* tells the story of one of the greatest thinkers of the 20th century, as well as the basics of his Theory of Relativity.

Trade paper, 112 pages
ISBN: 978-1-61373-865-8
$9.99 (CAN $12.99)
Ages 7 to 10

Newton
and the Antigravity Formula

In the late 1600s, science was still in its infancy. But that changed in 1687 when professor Isaac Newton published a book describing three laws of motion as well as a theory of universal gravitation. He also came up with a brand new field of mathematics, called calculus, to explain it all. The same equations that described the motion of a falling apple could also be used to describe the orbit of planets around the sun. It was revolutionary! *Newton and the Antigravity Formula* tells the story of the man who launched the field of modern physics and changed the way humans look at the world around them.

Trade paper, 112 pages
ISBN: 978-1-61373-861-0
$9.99 (CAN $12.99)
Ages 7 to 10

FL*SHES / OF GENIUS

Leonardo da Vinci
and the Pen That Drew the Future

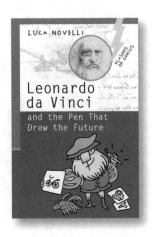

Like nobody before or since, Leonardo da Vinci united both
the arts and the sciences. He was not only a painter and skilled
draftsman, but also an inventor and tireless researcher. His art,
including the *Mona Lisa* and *The Last Supper*, remain classic of
Western civilization. And though he lived 500 years ago, many of his
futuristic ideas, such as the contact lens and the armored vehicle, are
still with us today. *Leonardo da Vinci and the Pen That Drew
the Future* tells the story of the greatest thinker of
the Renaissance.

Trade paper, 112 pages
ISBN: 978-1-61373-869-6
$9.99 (CAN $12.99)
Ages 7 to 10